# Enrichment
## MATH

Dear Student,

Here is your Enrichment Math book. This book is filled with exciting math things to do at home. You will play games, work puzzles, have trivia quizzes and contests. Ask your family and friends to work with you on these activities.

While you are having fun, you will be learning math. We hope Enrichment Math will be one of your favorite things to do this year.

Good luck from your friends at Enrichment Math.

*Peggy Kaye*
*Carole Greenes*
*Linda Schulman*

Enrichment Series Copyright © 1991 SRA/McGraw-Hill

# Table of Contents

Pages

**Whole Numbers**

- 3  The Case of the Missing Sign
- 4  Palindromes
- 5  The Greatest
- 6  The Big Difference
- 7  Line Up
- 8  Product Line
- 9  Cross-Number Puzzle
- 10 Beehive
- 11 Charge It
- 12 Average Facts
- 13 Quotient Match
- 14 Estimating Quotients
- 15 Number Search
- 16 Pick and Score

**Fractions**

- 17 World Capitals
- 18 Concentrate
- 19 Boxing Fractions
- 20 Fraction Toss
- 21 Fraction Squares
- 22 Fraction Subtracto
- 23 Number Facts
- 24 Toss a Fraction
- 25 Up and To The Right
- 26 Trivial Facts
- 27 Taking Chances
- 28 Number Please?

**Decimals**

- 29 Riddle Fever
- 30 Decimal Tic-Tac-Toe
- 31 Decimal Detective
- 32 Close to the Target
- 33 The Way to Go

Pages

- 34 Invention Time Line
- 35 Decimal Towers
- 36 Decimal Duel
- 37 Missing Points
- 38 Decimals in a Line
- 39 Match Up
- 40 Fast Ball

**Geometry and Measurement**

- 41 Measure Up
- 42 Metric Maze
- 43 Measurement Comparisons
- 44 Body Measures
- 45 Hidden Figures
- 46 Geo-Puzzle
- 47 Picture Puzzle
- 48 Size It
- 49 The Birthday Presents
- 50 Box It
- 51 Building Figures
- 52 Space Figures

**Problem Solving**

- 53 Drawing Conclusions
- 54 Picaria
- 55 Don't Lose Balance
- 56 Star Sum
- 57 Budget Time
- 58 Day By Day
- 59 Penny's Payroll
- 60 Likely Letters
- 61 Tree Diagrams
- 62 Menu Matters
- 63 Treasure Map
- 64 Model Room

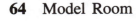

NAME

# The Case Of The Missing Sign

LESSON 1

Put in an addition sign to make each sentence true.

1. 4  8  6  5  9  3 = 1,079
2. 7  9  5  6  2  0  1 = 6,996
3. 9  4  3  2  9 = 9,441
4. 3  2  6  8  7  8 = 3,346
5. 8  2  6  7  3  2  1 = 8,147
6. 2  0  4  7  5  1  7  7 = 7,224
7. 3  4  2  8  6  5  9  0 = 10,018
8. 3  7  6  8  9  4  2 = 68,979
9. 8  4  9  2  6  4  8  5 = 85,411
10. 3  2  8  6  5  3  2  1  6 = 56,502
11. 1  0  4  7  3  9  5  2  0 = 40,567
12. 2  6  4  3  9  3  8  6  4  3 = 65,082

*Using Addition*

3

# Palindromes

A **palindrome** reads the same forward as backward.
The word *radar* is a palindrome.
The number 3,443 is a palindrome.

You can start with any number and make a palindrome.
Follow these steps.

**Step 1:** Pick a number.
**Step 2:** Reverse the number.
**Step 3:** Add the numbers.
**Step 4:** Repeat steps 2 and 3 until you get a palindrome.

```
   58
+  85
  143

+ 341
  484
```

Work with a member of your family.
Take turns thinking of a number and making it into a palindrome.
Show the work to make three palindromes.

Think of words you know that are palindromes.
Write as many as you can.

*Using Addition*

NAME _____

# The Greatest

LESSON 2

Subtract. The answer is a world record.

1.  4,124
   − 3,954   The greatest number of chin-ups without stopping.

2.  8,650
   − 4,793   The greatest number of push-ups without stopping.

3.  23,036
   − 10,540   The greatest number of rope jumps in one hour.

4.  57,904
   − 49,563   The greatest number of somersaults without stopping.

5.  40,607
   − 19,009   The greatest number of leg raises without stopping.

6.  91,835
   − 56,584   The greatest number of two-arm push-ups without stopping.

7.  82,513
   − 37,486   The greatest number of jumping jacks without stopping.

8.  79,714
   −  6,968   The greatest number of sit-ups without stopping.

*Using Subtraction*

5

# The Big Difference

Play this game with a friend.

**You will need:**

- Two sets of number cards, one set for each player.

**Number Cards**

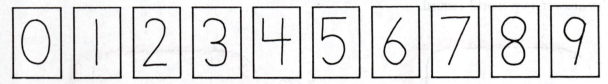

- Subtraction boxes for each player.

**Subtraction Boxes**

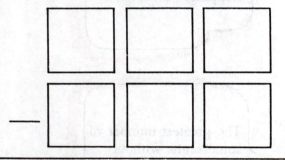

**On each round:**

- Each player mixes up a set of number cards, places them face down in a pile, and draws 6 cards.

- Each player writes one of the six numbers in each box and subtracts.

- The player with the greater difference scores one point.

**After five rounds, the player with the greatest score is the winner.**

Using Subtraction

NAME _____

# Line Up

LESSON 3

Here are four number lines.

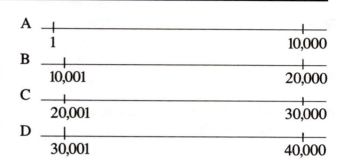

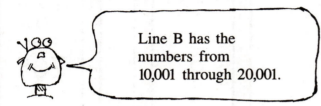

Line B has the numbers from 10,001 through 20,001.

Which line has the point for the product?

1. ____  676
         × 8

2. ____  259
         × 4

3. ____  900
         × 6

4. ____  813
         × 2

5. ____  1,523
         × 9

6. ____  5,781
         × 5

7. ____  1,802
         × 7

8. ____  9,145
         × 9

9. ____  4,098
         × 8

10. ____  7,764
          × 4

11. ____  2,966
          × 2

12. ____  3,073
          × 5

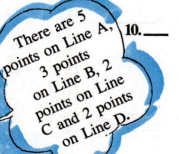

There are 5 points on Line A, 3 points on Line B, 2 points on Line C and 2 points on Line D.

*Multiplying by a 1-Digit Number*

7

# Product Line

This is a game for you and a friend.

**To play:**

- Take turns.
- Pick one number from Sign A and one number from Sign B.
- Multiply the numbers.
- Mark the product on the gameboard with your **X** or **O**.

The first players with four **X**s or **O**s in a row, column, or diagonal is the winner.

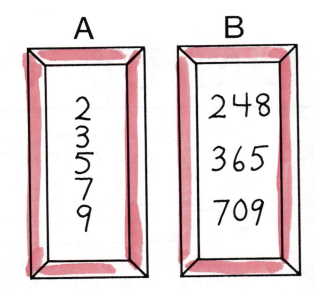

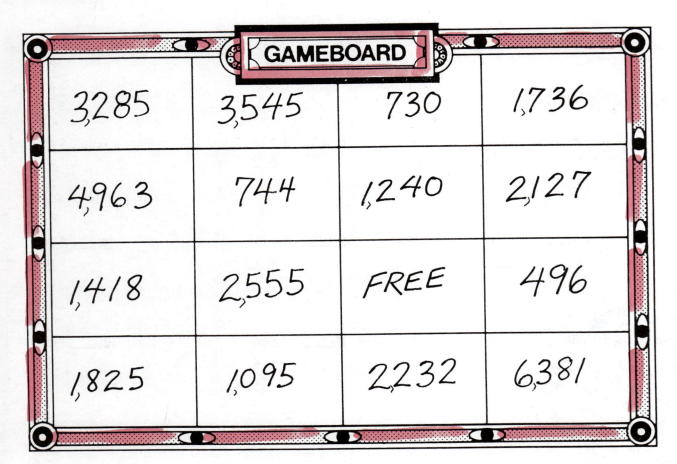

Multiplying by a 1-Digit Number

NAME

# Cross-Number Puzzle

**LESSON 4**

Multiply.
Write the product in the cross-number puzzle.

**ACROSS**

1. 825 × 150
5. 581 × 36
7. 26 × 3
8. 11 × 9
10. 689 × 30
11. 15 × 4
12. 283 × 144
13. 27 × 9
14. 56 × 14

**DOWN**

2. 400 × 500
3. 882 × 807
4. 127 × 7
6. 850 × 80
9. 291 × 324
10. 167 × 16

*Multiplying by 2- and 3-Digit Numbers*

9

# Beehive

This is a game for two teams.
One team is the **X** team.
The other team is the **O** team.

**Rules:**

- Take turns.
- Pick a number from each sign.
- Multiply the numbers.
- If the answer is on the gameboard, mark your **X** or **O** on the answer.

**The winner is the first team to make a path connecting its two sides of the gameboard.**

**Gameboard**

Team X side: 8,240; 12,600; 20,080; 14,100; 30,120; 14,700; 36,040; 72,080; 2,060; 7,210; 10,040; 18,020; 42,300; 54,060; 49,350; 4,200; 63,070; 28,200; 56,400; 35,140; 16,800; 6,180; 4,120; 40,160; 8,400

10        *Multiplying by 2- and 3-Digit Numbers*

NAME _____

# Charge It

**LESSON 5**

IN WHAT YEAR WERE PLASTIC CREDIT CARDS FIRST ISSUED IN THE UNITED STATES?

THE YEAR WAS ____  ____  ____  ____ .

**1.**

4)156    2)184

The only digit that is in both answers is _____ .
Write this digit in the hundreds place of the year.

**2.**

3)420    9)639

The only digit that is in both answers is _____ .
Write this digit in the ones place of the year.

**3.**

5)715    8)1,728

The only digit that is in both answers is _____ .
Write this digit in the thousands place of the year.

**4.**

6)630    7)2,275

The only digit that is in both answers is _____ .
Write this digit in the tens place of the year.

*Dividing by a 1-Digit Number*

11

# Average Facts

This is an activity for you and three friends.

For each person, record the:
- number of letters in the entire name (first, middle and last).
- height in inches.
- age in months.
- number of heart beats in one minute.

Find the averages by dividing the totals by 4.

| Name | Number of Letters in Name | Height (in inches) | Age (in months) | Number of Heart Beats (per minute) |
|---|---|---|---|---|
| 1. | | | | |
| 2. | | | | |
| 3. | | | | |
| 4. | | | | |
| Total | | | | |
| Average | | | | |

Whose height is closest to the average height? _____

Whose number of heart beats is closest to the average number of heart beats? _____

Dividing by a 1-Digit Number

NAME _____

# Quotient Match

LESSON 6

Estimate the quotient to match the football with the helmet.
Write the correct football letter under each helmet.

1.
31)93
_____

2.
22)880
_____

3.
70)910
_____

4.
11)792
_____

5.
58)1,798
_____

6.
15)1,305
_____

7.
93)2,046
_____

8.
79)4,582
_____

K  58

T 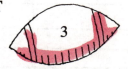 3

C 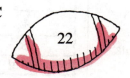 22

L 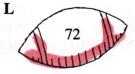 72

A 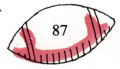 87

I 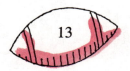 13

B 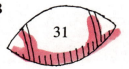 31

A 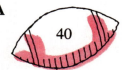 40

*Dividing by a 2-Digit Number*

# Estimating Quotients

This is a game for two players.
Take turns.

On each turn.
- Pick a division example.
- Estimate the quotient.
- Use paper and pencil or a calculator to check your estimate.
- Cross out the example.
- Find your score.

When all of the division examples are crossed out, add to find your total score.

**The winner is the player with the greater score.**

| 82)8,118 | 43)1,677 | 18)864 | 80)6,480 | 62)868 |
| 56)3,584 | 49)4459 | 98)7,056 | 11)561 | 32)800 |

If your quotient is between
10 and 30 score 4 points
30 and 50 score 3 points
50 and 70 score 5 points
70 and 90 score 2 points
90 and 100 score 6 points

| Round | Player 1 | Player 2 |
|---|---|---|
| 1 | | |
| 2 | | |
| 3 | | |
| 4 | | |
| 5 | | |
| Total | | |

*Dividing by a 2-Digit Number*

NAME

# Number Search

**LESSON 7**

Read the word name.
Find the number on the number board.
Look **down**, **across**, and **diagonally**.
Numbers may overlap.
Circle the number.

1. Three hundred sixty-four thousand, two hundred eighty-three

2. Eighty-seven million, two hundred eighty-four thousand, two hundred thirty-seven

3. Two million, four hundred thousand, seven hundred eighty-seven

4. Five million, four hundred twenty-six thousand, three hundred ninety-five

5. Four million, eight hundred seven thousand, forty-eight

6. Ten thousand, four hundred seventy-two

7. Seven million, three hundred eighty-seven thousand, seven hundred

8. Eight hundred seventy-two million, nine hundred fifty-one thousand, four hundred twenty-six

9. Forty-eight thousand, ninety-seven

10. Sixty-nine million, thirty-eight thousand, seven hundred ninety-five

**Number Board**

| 4 | 8 | 7 | 2 | 9 | 5 | 1 | 4 | 2 | 6 |
|---|---|---|---|---|---|---|---|---|---|
| 8 | 7 | 3 | 4 | 2 | 0 | 0 | 8 | 3 | 9 |
| 7 | 2 | 3 | 8 | 8 | 1 | 4 | 0 | 6 | 0 |
| 2 | 6 | 9 | 8 | 1 | 0 | 2 | 0 | 4 | 3 |
| 8 | 4 | 8 | 7 | 7 | 4 | 9 | 5 | 2 | 8 |
| 4 | 2 | 4 | 0 | 0 | 7 | 8 | 7 | 8 | 7 |
| 2 | 0 | 8 | 4 | 6 | 2 | 0 | 3 | 3 | 9 |
| 3 | 4 | 6 | 1 | 5 | 3 | 2 | 0 | 9 | 5 |
| 7 | 9 | 0 | 5 | 4 | 2 | 6 | 3 | 9 | 5 |

*Using Place Value to Millions*

15

# Pick And Score

Play this game with a member of your family.

Make a set of these cards for each player.

**Rules:**
- Take turns.
- Mix up the set of 9 cards.
- Turn the cards over in order to make a 9-digit number.
- Write the number on the line below.
- Score the number.

|  | NUMBER | SCORE |
|---|---|---|
| **Player 1:** |  |  |
| **Player 2:** |  |  |

Score 1 point for each of the following that is true.

- The number is greater than six hundred million.
- The digit in the ten millions place is greater than 3.
- The digit in the ones place is less than 5.
- The digit in the one millions place is an odd number.
- The digit in the hundred thousands place is an even number.
- The digit in the ten thousands place is 2.

**The winner is the player with the greater score.**

*Using Place Value to Millions*

NAME _____

# World Capitals

LESSON 8

Try to match each country with its capital.

Draw a line to match each mixed number with its improper fraction. The matching improper fraction gives the capital for the country. Score 1 point for each correct match on your list.

1. India  $1\frac{2}{3}$        $\frac{11}{6}$  Oslo

2. France  $2\frac{1}{5}$        $\frac{27}{8}$  Madrid

3. Spain  $3\frac{3}{8}$        $\frac{5}{3}$  New Delhi

4. Norway  $1\frac{5}{6}$        $\frac{11}{5}$  Paris

5. Argentina  $1\frac{6}{7}$        $\frac{11}{4}$  Tokyo

6. Japan  $2\frac{3}{4}$        $\frac{13}{7}$  Buenos Aires

7. Hungary  $3\frac{1}{3}$        $\frac{15}{7}$  Canberra

8. Greece  $4\frac{1}{6}$        $\frac{10}{3}$  Budapest

9. Italy  $1\frac{4}{5}$        $\frac{23}{8}$  Peking

10. Australia  $2\frac{1}{7}$        $\frac{9}{5}$  Rome

11. China  $2\frac{7}{8}$        $\frac{25}{6}$  Athens

How many points did you score? _____

*Using Mixed Numbers and Improper Fractions*

# Concentrate

This is a game for you and a friend.
Make these 10 improper fraction cards.

**Improper Fractions**

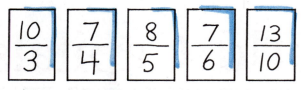

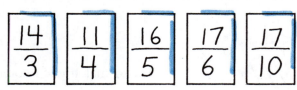

Make these 10 mixed number cards.

**Mixed Numbers**

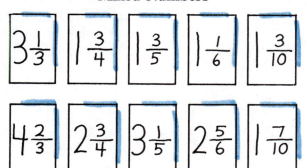

**To Play:**

- Mix up the 20 cards and lay them face down in four rows with five cards in each row.
- Take turns.
- Turn over two cards.
  If the improper fraction matches the mixed number, keep the cards.
  If the cards do not match, turn them over.

**After each player has had four turns, the player with the greater number of cards is the winner.**

Using Mixed Numbers and Improper Fractions

NAME _____

# Boxing Fractions

LESSON 9

Put one number in each box to make a true sentence.

Use all of the numbers.

**1.** Use 1, 1, 2, 3.

$\dfrac{\Box}{\Box} + \dfrac{\Box}{\Box} = \dfrac{5}{6}$

**2.** Use 1, 2, 3, 4.

$\dfrac{\Box}{\Box} + \dfrac{\Box}{\Box} = \dfrac{5}{4}$

**3.** Use 1, 1, 3, 5.

$\dfrac{\Box}{\Box} + \dfrac{\Box}{\Box} = \dfrac{8}{15}$

**4.** Use 1, 3, 5, 10.

$\dfrac{\Box}{\Box} + \dfrac{\Box}{\Box} = \dfrac{7}{10}$

**5.** Use 2, 3, 3, 4.

$\dfrac{\Box}{\Box} \quad \dfrac{\Box}{\Box} = \dfrac{17}{12}$

**6.** Use 1, 3, 9, 10.

$\dfrac{\Box}{\Box} \quad \dfrac{\Box}{\Box} = \dfrac{23}{20}$

**7.** Use 1, 6, 7, 8.

$\dfrac{\Box}{\Box} \quad \dfrac{\Box}{\Box} = \dfrac{25}{24}$

**8.** Use 2, 5, 6, 9.

$\dfrac{\Box}{\Box} \quad \dfrac{\Box}{\Box} = \dfrac{19}{18}$

*Adding Fractions with Unlike Denominators*

# Fraction Toss

Play this game with a friend.

**Rules:**

- Take turns.
- Toss two coins onto the playing board.
- Add the numbers.
- Score the sum.

After five rounds, the player with the greater number of points is the winner.

**Scoring**

- 2 points if the sum is 1 or more.
- 1 point if the sum is less than 1.

## Playing Board

| | | | |
|---|---|---|---|
| $\frac{1}{3}$ | $\frac{1}{5}$ | $\frac{7}{10}$ | $\frac{1}{8}$ |
| $\frac{3}{4}$ | $\frac{5}{6}$ | $\frac{2}{3}$ | $\frac{3}{5}$ |
| $\frac{8}{9}$ | $\frac{7}{8}$ | $\frac{11}{12}$ | $\frac{1}{6}$ |
| $\frac{3}{8}$ | $\frac{1}{4}$ | $\frac{2}{5}$ | $\frac{5}{8}$ |

| | Player | Player |
|---|---|---|
| Round 1 | | |
| Round 2 | | |
| Round 3 | | |
| Round 4 | | |
| Round 5 | | |
| Total | | |

*Adding Fractions with Unlike Denominators*

NAME _____

# Fraction Squares

**LESSON 10**

Subtract **across** and **down**.
Reduce the answers to lowest terms.
Write the answers in the squares.

1.

| $\frac{7}{8}$ | − | $\frac{3}{8}$ | = | |
|---|---|---|---|---|
| − | | − | | − |
| $\frac{1}{4}$ | − | $\frac{1}{8}$ | = | |
| = | | = | | = |
| | − | | = | |

2.

| $\frac{9}{10}$ | − | $\frac{2}{5}$ | = | |
|---|---|---|---|---|
| − | | − | | − |
| $\frac{3}{10}$ | − | $\frac{1}{5}$ | = | |
| = | | = | | = |
| | − | | = | |

3.

| $\frac{2}{3}$ | − | $\frac{1}{5}$ | = | |
|---|---|---|---|---|
| − | | − | | − |
| $\frac{2}{5}$ | − | $\frac{1}{15}$ | = | |
| = | | = | | = |
| | − | | = | |

4.

| $\frac{3}{4}$ | − | $\frac{1}{3}$ | = | |
|---|---|---|---|---|
| − | | − | | − |
| $\frac{1}{2}$ | − | $\frac{1}{6}$ | = | |
| = | | = | | = |
| | − | | = | |

*Subtracting Fractions with Unlike Denominators*

# Fraction Subtracto

Find someone to play this game with you.
Make these cards.
Mix up the cards and place them face down.

**Rules:**
- Take turns.
- Pick a card. Write the number in one of the squares below.
- Score one point for making a true statement.
- After all the cards have been used, the player with the greater number of points is the winner.

☐ > $\frac{1}{3}$  ☐ < $\frac{5}{6}$

☐ < $\frac{1}{2}$  ☐ > $\frac{1}{2}$

☐ − $\frac{1}{6}$ > $\frac{1}{4}$  ☐ − $\frac{1}{4}$ < $\frac{5}{12}$

1 − ☐ < $\frac{1}{2}$  1 − ☐ > $\frac{1}{2}$

☐ − ☐ < $\frac{7}{12}$  ☐ − ☐ > $\frac{1}{6}$

**The winner is** _____ .

22

*Subtracting Fractions with Unlike Denominators*

NAME _____

# Number Facts

LESSON 11

Fill in the blanks.

1. The number of countries in South America is equal to $\frac{1}{3}$ of 39, or _____ .

2. The number of strings on a violin is equal to $\frac{2}{7}$ of 14, or _____ .

3. The number of U.S. Presidents before Lincoln is equal to $\frac{3}{4}$ of 20, or _____ .

4. The number of provinces in Canada is equal to $\frac{5}{8}$ of 16, or _____ .

5. The number of U.S. Senators is equal to $\frac{1}{10}$ of 1,000, or _____ .

6. The number of stories in the Empire State Building is equal to $\frac{2}{3}$ of 153, or _____ .

7. The number of cards in a regular deck is equal to $\frac{1}{2}$ of 104, or _____ .

8. The number of pencils in a gross is equal to $\frac{3}{5}$ of 240, or _____ .

9. The number of home runs hit by Hank Aaron is equal to $\frac{5}{6}$ of 906, or _____ .

10. The number of calories in a peanut butter and jelly sandwich is equal to $\frac{11}{12}$ of 300, or _____ .

*Multiplying a Fraction and a Whole Number*

# Toss A Fraction

This is a game for two players.
Get a coin.
Make these cards.

Rules
- Take turns.
- Pick a card and toss the coin.
- If the coin lands heads up, find one-half of the number on the card.
- If the coin lands tails up, find one-third of the number on the card.
- Write the answer on the score card.

The player with the greatest total score after six rounds is the winner.

84  36  18  30  54  72

24  48  66  12  78  60

**Score Card**

| Round | Player 1 | Player 2 |
|---|---|---|
| 1 | | |
| 2 | | |
| 3 | | |
| 4 | | |
| 5 | | |
| 6 | | |
| Total | | |

*Multiplying a Fraction and a Whole Number*

NAME _____

# Up And To The Right

LESSON 12

Follow the arrow directions.
Multiply up. Multiply across.
Complete the square.

1.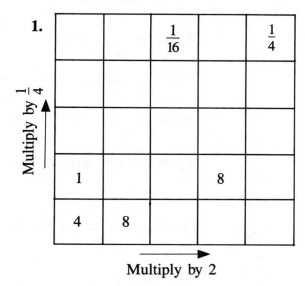

2.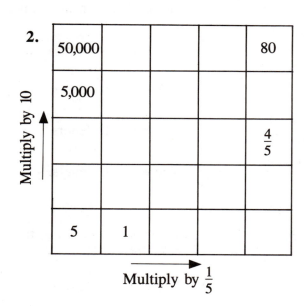

3.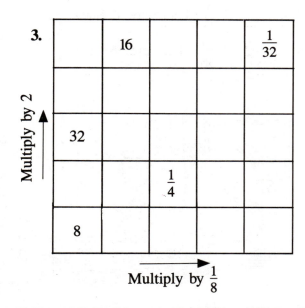

4.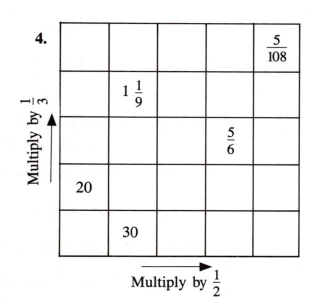

*Multiplying Fractions*  25

# Trivial Facts

This is a game for you and your family.
First, each player tries to answer the questions.
Then multiply to check the answers.
The product gives the answer to the question.
Ring the correct answer.
The winner is the one with the most correct answers.
There can be more than one winner.

1. $\frac{2}{3} \times \frac{4}{5} =$ How many letters are in the longest name of a state in the United States?

    $\frac{6}{8}$ There are 10 letters.

    $\frac{6}{15}$ There are 11 letters.

    $\frac{22}{15}$ There are 12 letters.

    $\frac{8}{15}$ There are 13 letters.

2. $\frac{1}{2} \times \frac{4}{5} =$ How many small squares are on a scrabble board?

    $\frac{5}{7}$ There are 64 small squares.

    $\frac{5}{10}$ There are 100 small squares.

    $\frac{2}{5}$ There are 225 small squares.

    $\frac{1}{2}$ There are 400 small squares.

3. $\frac{3}{10} \times \frac{5}{6} =$ How many letters are in the Greek alphabet?

    $\frac{1}{2}$ There are 32 letters.

    $\frac{15}{16}$ There are 28 letters.

    $\frac{8}{60}$ There are 26 letters.

    $\frac{1}{4}$ There are 24 letters.

4. $1\frac{3}{4} \times \frac{8}{9} =$ How many stars are in the Big Dipper?

    $1\frac{5}{9}$ There are 7 stars.

    $\frac{8}{9}$ There are 10 stars.

    $1\frac{2}{13}$ There are 12 stars.

    $1\frac{23}{36}$ There are 16 stars.

5. $2\frac{1}{8} \times 2 =$ How old was Christopher Columbus when he first arrived in the New World?

    $4\frac{1}{8}$ Columbus was 24 years old.

    $4\frac{1}{4}$ Columbus was 41 years old.

    $2\frac{1}{16}$ Columbus was 53 years old.

    $2\frac{1}{4}$ Columbus was 62 years old.

*Multiplying Fractions and Mixed Numbers*

NAME _____

# Taking Chances

LESSON 13

You have this bag of blocks.
With your eyes closed, you pick a block.
What is the probability that you will pick:

1. ▨ ? _____

2. ▩ ? _____

3. ⬤ ? _____

4. ⬤ or ▩ ? _____

5. ⬤ or ▨ ? _____

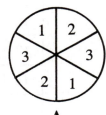   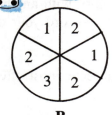   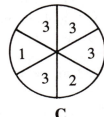

    A                  B                 C

Identify the spinner.

6. The probability of spinning a 2 is $\frac{2}{6}$. _____

7. The probability of spinning a 32 is $\frac{1}{6}$. _____

8. There is an equal probabilty of spinning a 1 or a 2. _____

Which spinner would you choose?

9. You win if you spin a 3. _____

10. You win if you spin a 2. _____

11. You win if you spin a 2 or a 3. _____

12. You win if you spin a 1 or a 2. _____

*Using Probability*

# Number Please?

Work with someone in your family.

- Choose 50 telephone numbers from your telephone book.
- Add the first and last digits of each number.
- Make a tally mark for each sum in Table 1.
- Find the total number for each sum.

1. Which sum occurred most often?

   _____

2. What is the probability that given any telephone number, the sum of the first and last digits will be the sum you gave in Exercise 1?

   _____

Check out the probability with another 50 telephone numbers. Record your data in Table 2.

3. Did the same sum occur most often?

   _____

|     | TABLE 1 |       |     | TABLE 2 |       |
|-----|---------|-------|-----|---------|-------|
| Sum | Tally   | Total | Sum | Tally   | Total |
| 2   |         |       | 2   |         |       |
| 3   |         |       | 3   |         |       |
| 4   |         |       | 4   |         |       |
| 5   |         |       | 5   |         |       |
| 6   |         |       | 6   |         |       |
| 7   |         |       | 7   |         |       |
| 8   |         |       | 8   |         |       |
| 9   |         |       | 9   |         |       |
| 10  |         |       | 10  |         |       |
| 11  |         |       | 11  |         |       |
| 12  |         |       | 12  |         |       |
| 13  |         |       | 13  |         |       |
| 14  |         |       | 14  |         |       |
| 15  |         |       | 15  |         |       |
| 16  |         |       | 16  |         |       |
| 17  |         |       | 17  |         |       |
| 18  |         |       | 18  |         |       |

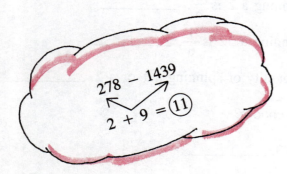

*Using Probability*

# Riddle Fever

**LESSON 14**

**WHY SHOULDN'T YOU TELL A SECRET TO A PIG?**

Write the decimal equivalent.

Then write the letter of the fraction on the line above its decimal equivalent.

I  $\frac{1}{2}$ = ____   C  $\frac{6}{10}$ = ____   L  $\frac{85}{100}$ = ____   T  $\frac{1}{5}$ = ____

A  $\frac{1}{4}$ = ____   Q  $\frac{3}{4}$ = ____   E  $\frac{9}{50}$ = ____   A  $\frac{1}{10}$ = ____

I  $\frac{3}{10}$ = ____   B  $\frac{16}{20}$ = ____   E  $\frac{7}{10}$ = ____   S  $\frac{4}{25}$ = ____

W  $\frac{1}{25}$ = ____   L  $\frac{23}{50}$ = ____   U  $\frac{2}{100}$ = ____   E  $\frac{3}{20}$ = ____

U  $\frac{2}{5}$ = ____   L  $\frac{18}{20}$ = ____   S  $\frac{6}{25}$ = ____

**YOU SHOULDN'T TELL A SECRET TO A PIG**

$\overline{0.8}$  $\overline{0.18}$  $\overline{0.6}$  $\overline{0.1}$  $\overline{0.4}$  $\overline{0.16}$  $\overline{0.15}$  $\overline{0.5}$  $\overline{0.2}$

$\overline{0.04}$  $\overline{0.3}$  $\overline{0.9}$  $\overline{0.46}$  $\overline{0.24}$  $\overline{0.75}$  $\overline{0.02}$  $\overline{0.7}$  $\overline{0.25}$  $\overline{0.85}$

*Changing Fractions to Decimals*

# Decimal Tic-Tac-Toe

Play this game with a friend.

**How to Play**

- Take turns.
- Pick a number from the sign.
- Mark the decimal equivalent on the gameboard with your **X** or **O**.
- Cross off the number on the sign.

The first player with four **X**s or **O**s in a row, column, or diagonal is the winner.

| $\frac{1}{2}$ | $\frac{1}{5}$ | $\frac{2}{5}$ | $\frac{3}{5}$ |
|---|---|---|---|
| $\frac{4}{5}$ | $\frac{3}{10}$ | $\frac{7}{10}$ | $\frac{9}{10}$ |
| $\frac{1}{4}$ | $\frac{3}{4}$ | $\frac{7}{20}$ | $\frac{11}{20}$ |
| $\frac{1}{50}$ | $\frac{12}{25}$ | $\frac{3}{50}$ | $\frac{81}{100}$ |

## GAMEBOARD

| 0.8 | 0.25 | 0.7 | 0.06 |
|---|---|---|---|
| 0.02 | 0.5 | 0.35 | 0.75 |
| 0.48 | 0.81 | 0.6 | 0.2 |
| 0.4 | 0.9 | 0.55 | 0.3 |

*Changing Fractions to Decimals*

NAME _____

# Decimal Detective

LESSON 15

Use the clues to find the number in the cloud.
Draw a ring around the number.

1.

- Each digit is an odd number.
- The digit in the tenths place is the greatest digit.
- The digit in the hundredths place is 3.

2.

- The number is greater than 26.3
- The digit in the tens place is 3 more than the digit in the tenths place.
- The digit in the ones place is not 6.

3.

- Rounded to the nearest whole number, the number is 24.
- The digit in the hundredths place is 7.
- The digit in the tenths place is 3.

4.

- The digit in the tenths place is 8.
- Each digit is different.
- The sum of the digits is 16.
- The digit in the hundredths place is 6.

5. 

- Each digit is even.
- The digit in the hundredths place is 2.
- The digit in the thousandths place is 4.
- The digit in the tenths place is 8.

6.

- Each digit is different.
- The number is greater than 3.1.
- The digit in the hundredths place is 7.
- The digit in the thousandths place is odd.

*Using Decimals to Thousandths*

# Close To The Target

This is a game for you and a friend.
Make these cards.
Mix up the cards and place them face down.

**Rules:**

■ Take turns turning over a card.
■ Both players write the digit shown on the card
  in one of their 10 boxes.
■ When the boxes are filled, players put in a
  decimal point in each of their three numbers.
■ Compare each player's number to the target number.
  Ring the one that is closer.
The player with the most ringed
numbers is the winner.

| **Player 1** | **Target Number** | **Player 2** |
|:---:|:---:|:---:|
| □ □ □ | 10 | □ □ □ |
| □ □ □ | 3 | □ □ □ |
| □ □ □ □ | 6 | □ □ □ □ |

**The winner is** _____ .

*Using Decimals to Thousandths*

NAME _____

# The Way To Go

LESSON 16

Write the decimal numbers on the lines from least to greatest.
Write the letter of each decimal number under the number.
The letters will spell the name of a vehicle.

1.  X   0.231   _____  _____  _____  _____
    I   0.406
    A   0.057
    T   0.009

2.  T   0.007   _____  _____  _____  _____  _____  _____
    N   0.6
    R   0.01
    I   0.299
    A   0.082

3.  L   0.018   _____  _____  _____  _____  _____  _____  _____  _____  _____
    R   0.005
    N   0.107
    P   0.016
    E   0.871
    A   0.097
    I   0.004
    A   0.001

*Comparing and Ordering Decimals*

33

# Invention Time Line

Work with someone in your family to find out when each of the items listed below was invented.

- Work together.
- Use a pencil.
- Write the name of the invention next to its date.

To check your answers, arrange the decimal numbers in order from least to greatest. The order of the decimals gives the order in which the items were invented.

| | |
|---|---|
| 0.02 | Carpet Sweeper |
| 0.003 | Match |
| 0.01 | Lawn Mower |
| 0.029 | Ballpoint Pen |
| 0.012 | Safety Pin |
| 0.42 | Long Playing Record |
| 0.412 | Automatic Toaster |
| 0.209 | Zipper |
| 0.294 | Air Conditioning |

| Invention | Date |
|---|---|
| | 1827 |
| | 1831 |
| | 1849 |
| | 1876 |
| | 1888 |
| | 1891 |
| | 1911 |
| | 1918 |
| | 1947 |

*Comparing and Ordering Decimals*

NAME _____

# Decimal Towers

Complete the decimal towers.
- Start at the bottom.
- Add two numbers that are side by side.
- Write the answer in the block above.

1.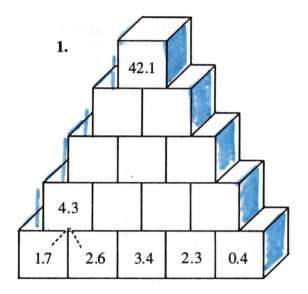

2.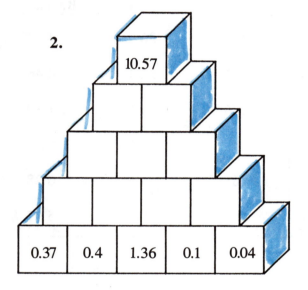

3.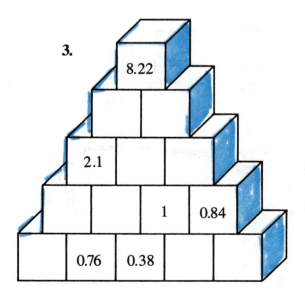

4.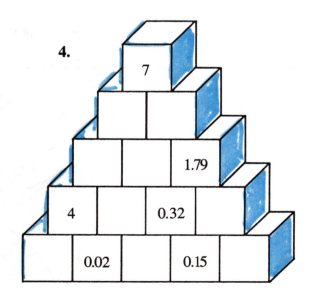

*Adding and Subtracting with Decimals*

# Decimal Duel

Play this game with a friend.

**Rules:**
- Take turns.
- Pick two numbers from the number board.
- Find the sum of the two numbers.
- Cross out the two numbers on the number board.
- Find the sum on the number line. Write the score for the sum.

When all of the numbers are crossed out, the player with the greater total score is the winner.

**Number Board**

| 25.4 | 36.4  | 43.27 | 50.2 |
|------|-------|-------|------|
| 6.32 | 52.1  | 0.46  | 3.26 |
| 4.86 | 24.6  | 1.39  | 11.7 |
| 3.4  | 12.06 | 21.52 | 23.3 |
| 9.63 | 34.3  | 0.28  | 13.9 |
| 17.1 | 49.5  | 5.97  | 0.98 |

| Player 1 | Player 2 |
|----------|----------|
|          |          |

←1 point→ ←2 points→ ←3 points→ ←4 points→ ←5 points→

0    20    40    60    80    100

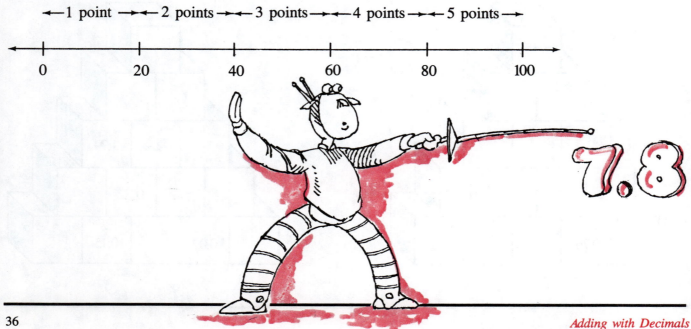

36  Adding with Decimals

# Missing Points

LESSON 18

A decimal point in each example is missing.
Estimate to write the decimal point in the correct place in the answer.
Complete the examples in each row.
Then find the total number of decimal places to the right of the decimal points in the answers.
Is the total the same as the check number for the row?

1.  2.6      2.  20.6     3.  5.5      4.  50.3     5.  6.28
   × 7          × 0.5        × 3.2        × 7.5        × 0.5
    182          103          176        37725          314

Check Number: 7

6.  7.6      7.  80.5     8.  24.5     9.  36.7    10.  1.3
   × 22         × 0.36       × 5.8        × 3.8        × 0.9
   1672         2898         1421        13946          117

Check Number: 8

11. 0.05    12.  3.48    13.  5.24    14.  2.56    15.  30.7
   × 36         × 0.5        × 6.5        × 10         × 14
     18          174         3406          256         4298

Check Number: 7

16.  340    17.  54.6    18.  98.5    19.  149.6   20.  25.25
   × 0.89       × 34.2       × 0.6        × 0.03       × 3.02
   3026        186732         591         4488         76255

Check Number: 10

*Multiplying with Decimals*

37

# Decimals In A Line

Here is a game for two players, player **X** and player **O**.

**Rules:**
- Take turns.
- Pick two numbers from the sign.
- Multiply the numbers.
- Mark the answer on the gameboard with your **X** or **O**.

The first player with four **X**s or **O**s in a row, column, or diagonal is the winner.

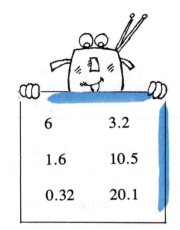

| 6 | 3.2 |
| 1.6 | 10.5 |
| 0.32 | 20.1 |

## GAMEBOARD

| 32.16 | 5.12 | 120.6 | 6.4312 |
|---|---|---|---|
| 1.024 | 3.36 | 16.8 | FREE |
| 0.512 | 3.36 | 19.2 | 211.05 |
| 33.6 | 64.32 | 63 | 9.6 |

The winner is _____ .

38    *Multiplying with Decimals*

NAME _____

# Match Up

LESSON 19

Match the divisors with the dividends
so that all the quotients are the same.
Write the divisor on the line.
Divide to check the quotient.

**Divisors**

2 3 4 5 6 7

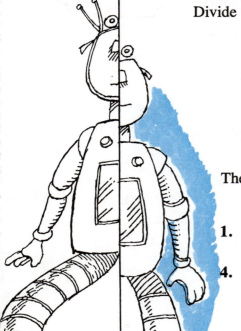

The quotient is 1.2.

1. ___)3.6   2. ___)2.4   3. ___)6.0

4. ___)7.2   5. ___)4.8   6. ___)8.4

**Divisors**

2 3 5 6 8 9

The quotient is 2.41.

7. ___)4.82   8. ___)21.69   9. ___)12.05

10. ___)14.46   11. ___)19.28   12. ___)7.23

*Dividing Decimals by Whole Numbers*

39

# Fast Ball

**NOLAN RYAN HOLDS THE RECORD AS THE FASTEST PITCHER. HOW FAST WAS HIS RECORD-SETTING PITCH?**

To answer this question, work with a friend.

- Take turns.
- Divide.
- Cross off the answers on the mitt.
- The number that is left is the speed of the ball.

*On the mitt:* 11.17, 9.69, 203.1, 8.12, 15.43, 100.9, 122.1, 68.4, 7.08

1. 3)609.3
2. 2)30.86
3. 5)610.5

4. 4)273.6
5. 6)58.14
6. 2)278.8

7. 7)49.56
8. 9)73.08
9. 8)89.36

**THE PITCH WAS MEASURED AT A SPEED OF _____ MILES PER HOUR.**

Dividing Decimals by Whole Numbers

NAME _____

# Measure Up

LESSON 20

This crayon is 6 centimeters long and weighs 12 grams.

Measure the length of each of these crayons.

Estimate the weight.

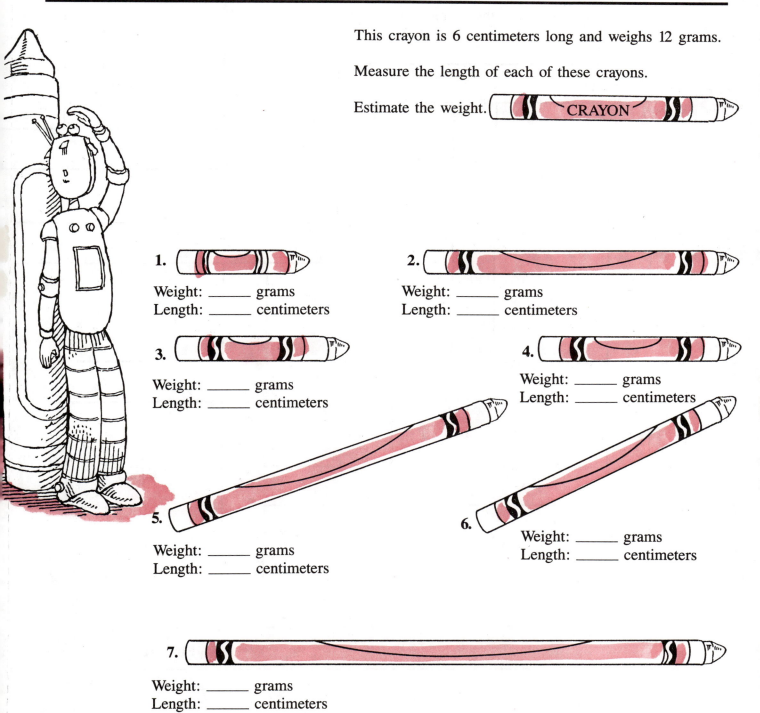

1.
Weight: _____ grams
Length: _____ centimeters

2.
Weight: _____ grams
Length: _____ centimeters

3.
Weight: _____ grams
Length: _____ centimeters

4.
Weight: _____ grams
Length: _____ centimeters

5.
Weight: _____ grams
Length: _____ centimeters

6.
Weight: _____ grams
Length: _____ centimeters

7.
Weight: _____ grams
Length: _____ centimeters

*Using Metric Units*

# Metric Maze

Follow the line.

Work with a friend.

Find the path from START to FINISH.

Measure the length of the path to the nearest centimeter.

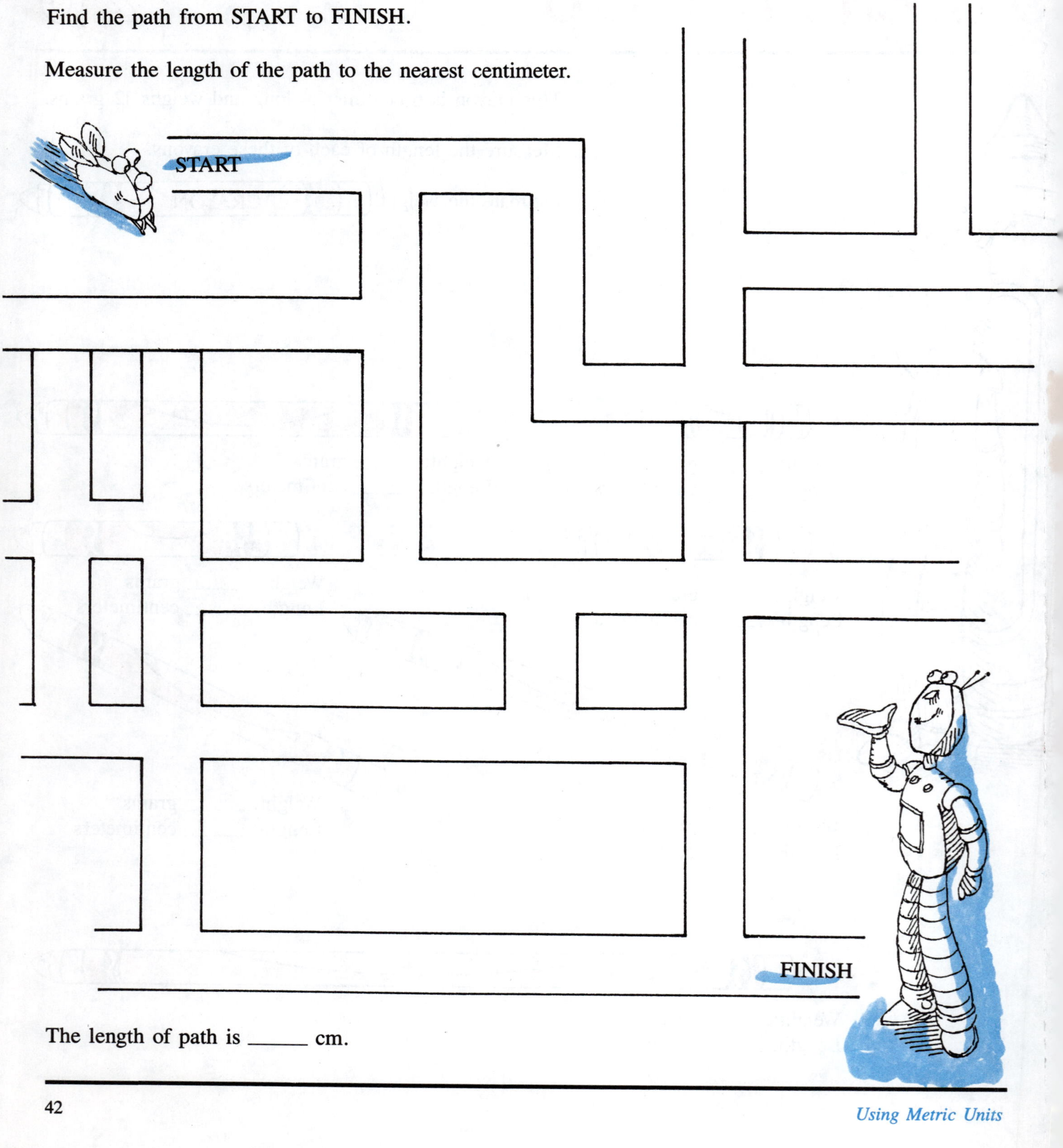

START

FINISH

The length of path is _____ cm.

42

*Using Metric Units*

NAME _____

# Measurement Comparisons

LESSON 21

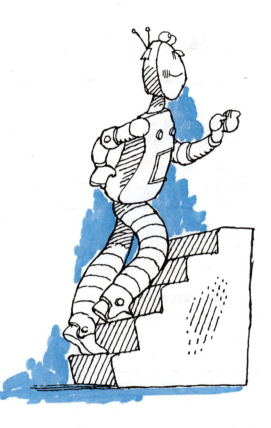

Compare the measures.

Write >, <, or = in each ◯.

1.  6 yd ◯ 18 ft
2.  40 in. ◯ 1 yd
3.  3 lb ◯ 33 oz
4.  4 pt ◯ 9 c
5.  2000 lb ◯ 1 T
6.  23 in. ◯ 2 ft
7.  2 c ◯ 1 pt
8.  8 qt ◯ 15 pt
9.  2 yd ◯ 60 in.
10. 3 qt ◯ 9 gal
11. 3 lb ◯ 60 oz
12. 16 oz ◯ 1 lb
13. 5 gal ◯ 18 qt
14. 10 ft ◯ 3 yd
15. 4 ft ◯ 48 in.
16. 5 pt ◯ 2 qt

Climb up one stair for each >. Climb down one stair for each <. Do not move for each =. If your answers are correct, you should end up at the top of the staircase.

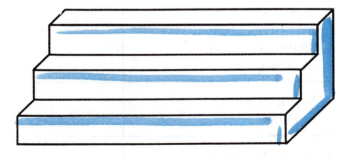

START

*Using Customary Units*

43

# Body Measures

Do this activity with someone in your family.
Estimate first.
Write your estimate. Then measure.

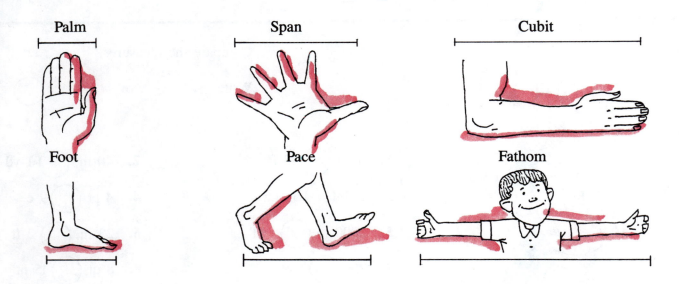

| What To Measure | Estimate | Measurement |
|---|---|---|
| length of your arm in palms | | |
| length of your leg in feet | | |
| length of a room in paces | | |
| length of a chair in cubits | | |
| length of a car in fathoms | | |
| length of a table in spans | | |

*Using Nonstandard Units*

NAME _____

# Hidden Figures

LESSON 22

Find the number of triangles and quadrilaterals in each figure.

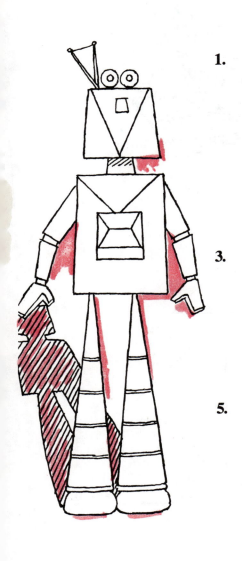

1.

   _____ triangles

   _____ quadrilaterals

2.

   _____ triangles

   _____ quadrilaterals

3.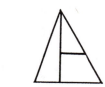

   _____ triangles

   _____ quadrilaterals

4.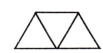

   _____ triangles

   _____ quadrilaterals

5.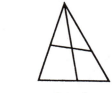

   _____ triangles

   _____ quadrilaterals

6.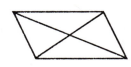

   _____ triangles

   _____ quadrilaterals

Did you find a total of 24 triangles and 12 quadrilaterals?

*Identifying Polygons*

45

# Geo-Puzzle

Ask someone in your family to do this activity with you.
Trace the figure below twice.
Cut along the lines.
Give each person a set of seven pieces.

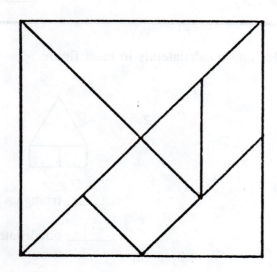

Try to make these pictures using the seven pieces.

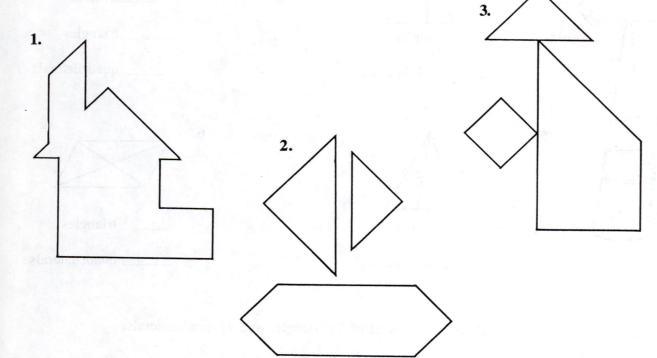

1.

2.

3.

46

**Using Polygons**

NAME

# Picture Puzzle

LESSON 23

Use the perimeter and area clues to identify each person's photograph. Write the name of the person under the photograph.

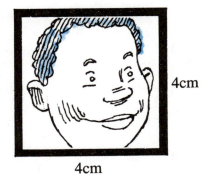

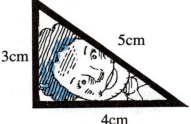

1. _____

2. _____

3. _____

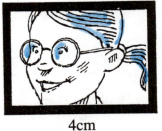

4. _____

5. _____

6. _____

**Elliot**
   Perimeter = 16 cm
   Area = 12 sq cm

**Rosa**
   Perimeter = 14 cm
   Area = 12 sq cm

**Jack**
   Perimeter = 12 cm
   Area = 9 sq cm

**Ben**
   Perimeter = 16 cm
   Area = 16 sq cm

**Sara**
   Perimeter = 12 cm
   Area = 6 sq cm

**Mele**
   Perimeter = 14 cm
   Area = 10 sq cm

*Finding Perimeter and Area Using Metric Units*

# Size It

Do this activity with someone in your family.

- Find pictures in books or magazines.
- Use a centimeter ruler to measure the length and width.
- Find the perimeter.
- Find the area.

1. Find a picture of a building.
   Length of picture _____ cm
   Width of picture _____ cm
   Perimeter _____ cm
   Area _____ sq cm

2. Find a picture of a person.
   Length of picture _____ cm
   Width of picture _____ cm
   Perimeter _____ cm
   Area _____ sq cm

3. Find a picture of a car.
   Length of picture _____ cm
   Width of picture _____ cm
   Perimeter _____ cm
   Area _____ sq cm

4. Find a picture of a flower.
   Length of picture _____ cm
   Width of picture _____ cm
   Perimeter _____ cm
   Area _____ sq cm

*Finding Perimeter and Area Using Metric Units*

NAME _____

# The Birthday Presents

LESSON 24

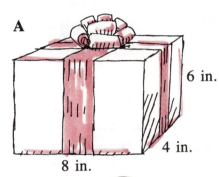

Identify each person's birthday present.
Fill in the blank with the letter of the box.

**1.** Eric
   "The volume of the box is 125 cubic inches.
   My present is in Box _____ ."

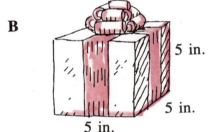

**2.** Pam
   "The volume of the box is 80 cubic inches.
   The height and width of the box are the same.
   My present is in Box _____ ."

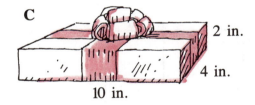

**3.** Sue
   "The volume of the box is 192 cubic inches.
   The length of the box is twice the width.
   My present is in Box _____ ."

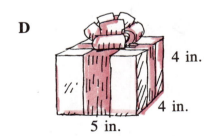

**4.** Jerry
   "The volume of the box is 80 cubic inches.
   The height of the box is half the width.
   My present is in Box _____ ."

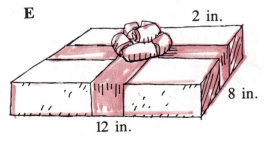

**5.** Allison
   "The volume of the box is 192 cubic inches.
   The length of the box is one foot.
   My present is in Box _____ ."

*Finding Volume Using Customary Units*

# Box It

This is an activity for you and your family.

- Find 4 boxes. Each box must be rectangular in shape.
- In the table below, write the names of the types of boxes in order by size.
  Make Box 1 be the box you think has the greatest volume.
  Make Box 4 be the box you think has the smallest volume.
- Measure the length, width and height of each box to the nearest inch. Record these measurements.
- Find the volume of each box.
- Ring the box with the greatest volume.

|  | Name | Length | Width | Height | Volume (cubic inches) |
|---|---|---|---|---|---|
| Box 1 |  |  |  |  |  |
| Box 2 |  |  |  |  |  |
| Box 3 |  |  |  |  |  |
| Box 4 |  |  |  |  |  |

Were you a good estimator?

Which box has the greatest volume? _____

Which box has the smallest volume? _____

Finding Volume Using Customary Units

NAME _____

# Building Figures

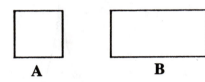
A               B

C

These shapes are used as faces to build the three-dimensional figures shown below. How many of each face are needed? Don't forget about the faces you cannot see. Always use the fewest number of faces possible.

1.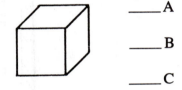
___ A
___ B
___ C

2.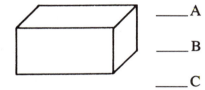
___ A
___ B
___ C

3.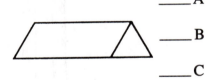
___ A
___ B
___ C

4.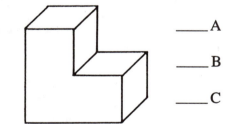
___ A
___ B
___ C

5.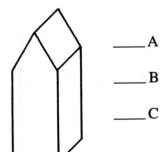
___ A
___ B
___ C

6.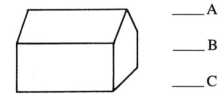
___ A
___ B
___ C

Check your totals:
A - 19
B - 20
C - 6

*Using Three-Dimensional Figures*

# Space Figures

Here are pictures of four space figures.

 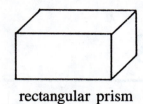  

cube    rectangular prism    sphere    cone

Ask an adult to help you with this activity.

- Get a magazine and a pair of scissors.
- Cut out pictures of objects suggested by each space figure.
- Tape the pictures below.
- Write the name of each figure below the picture.

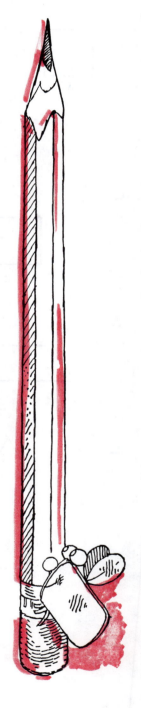

52

*Finding Three-Dimensional Figures*

NAME _____

# Drawing Conclusions

### LESSON 26

1. Barbara is taller than Nicole. Nicole is taller than Kimberly. Who is taller, Barbara or Kimberly?

   _____

2. My birthday is the day after tomorrow. Yesterday was Wednesday. On what day of the week is my birthday?

   _____

3. Matt, Jon, and Mario ran a race. Matt did not finish last. Mario finished first. Who finished last?

   _____

4. There are three children in a family. They are 5, 7, and 10 years old. Mike is the oldest. Kim is not younger than Edward. How old is Edward?

   _____

5. Samantha bought a ball, a bat, and a mitt. The prices were $11.50, $4.50 and $6.50. The mitt cost $5 more than the bat. What was the cost of the ball?

   _____

6. Mr. Phearson planted a row each of carrots, squash, and peppers. The peppers were planted to the right of the squash. The carrots were planted to the left of the squash. Which vegetable was planted just left of the peppers?

   _____

7. The movie was shown at 11:00 AM, 1:00 PM, 3:00 PM, 5:00 PM, and 7:00 PM. Mrs. Kelly went to see the movie before 3:00 PM. She did not see a morning show. At what time did Mrs. Kelly see the movie?

   _____

8. Tricia, Dan, Mia, and Pedro all work for the same company. Pedro has worked there the longest. Mia has worked there longer than Tricia and Dan. Dan has worked there longer than Tricia. Who has worked there the shortest amount of time?

   _____

*Using Thinking Skills*

# Picaria

Picaria is a game that was brought to the United States by Spanish settlers. It is a game for two players.

You need six game pieces, three for each player. You could use three coins and three beans.

**Rules:**
- Players take turns placing a game piece in a circle on the Picaria Board.

- When all six pieces have been placed, players take turns moving their pieces.

- On each turn a player moves one piece along a straight line to a circle without a piece.

The first player with three game pieces in a line is the winner.

**Picaria Board**

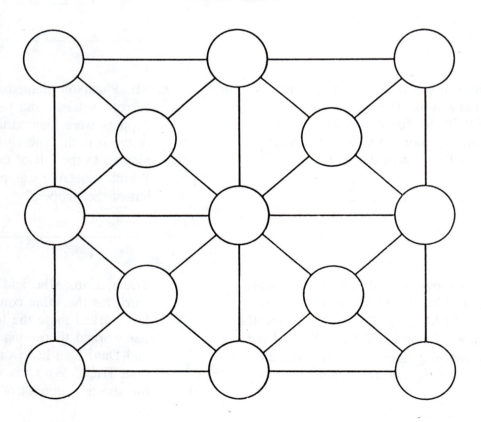

54

*Using Thinking Skills*

NAME _____

# Don't Lose Balance

LESSON 27

- Choose weights to put on the scales to make the scales balance.
- Write the numbers in the boxes.
- You may use a weight more than once.
- All of the measures are in ounces.

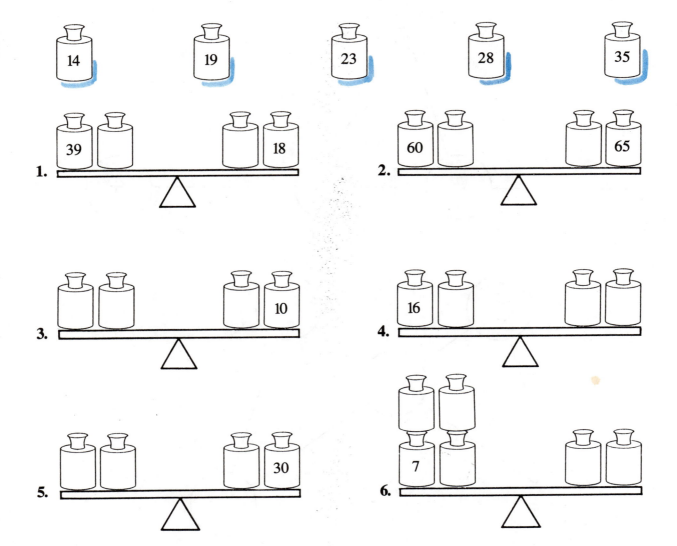

*Guessing and Checking*

55

# Star Sum

This is an activity for you and someone in your family. Work together.

- Use the numbers 1, 2, 3, 4, 8, 10 and 11.

- Put one number in each circle so that the four numbers in each line add to 28.

HINT
Put numbers on pieces of paper. Move the papers around and test the sums.

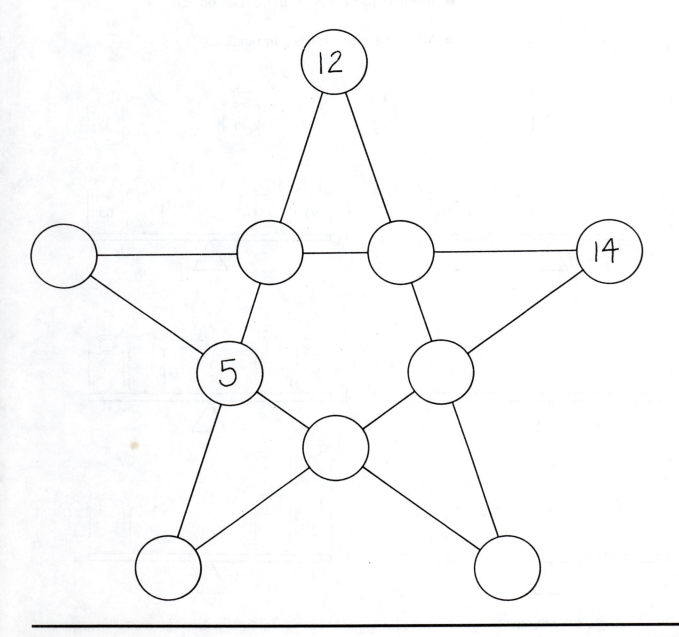

56     *Guessing and Checking*

# Budget Time

**LESSON 28**

Marcie earned $36 last month. The circle graph shows how Marcie spent her money.

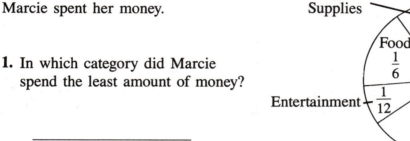

1. In which category did Marcie spend the least amount of money?

   _____

2. In which category did Marcie spend the most amount of money?

   _____

3. Name 2 categories in which Marcie spent half of her money.

   _____

4. Name 3 categories in which Marcie spent half of her money.

   _____

5. How much money did Marcie spend for food?

   _____

6. How much money did Marcie save?

   _____

7. How much more did Marcie spend for transportation than entertainment?

   _____

8. Altogether, how much money did Marcie spend for school supplies and food?

   _____

9. If Marcie spent the same amount of money for transportation each month, how much would she spend in one year?

   _____

*Using a Circle Graph*

# Day By Day

Have someone in your family help you think about how you spend your day.

Make a list of activities that you do.

Write down the number of hours you spend doing each activity.

| Activity | Number of Hours |
|---|---|
|  |  |

Here is a circle graph that is divided in 24 sections.
Each section stands for 1 hour.
Label the sections for the activities.

**My Day**

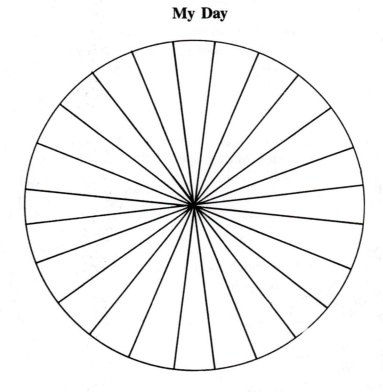

In which activity do you spend the most time each day? _____

58

*Making a Circle Graph*

NAME _____

# Penny's Payroll

LESSON 29

The Penny Power Company has its employees sign in and sign out at work. The company then computes how much to pay the employees based on the number of hours worked.

For work of more than 8 hours per day, a bonus of $3 per hour is paid for the overtime.

Complete the table. It might be helpful to use a calculator.

| Employee | Time In | Time Out | Total Number of Hours | Hourly Wage | Total Wage |
|---|---|---|---|---|---|
| 1. A. Barrons | 7:00AM | | 8 | $5.35 | $42.80 |
| 2. B. Cartright | 7:30AM | 1:30PM | 6 | $4.50 | |
| 3. C. Davenport | 7:00AM | 4:00PM | 9 | | $60.60 |
| 4. D. Elio | 8:00AM | 12:00PM | | $7.50 | $30.00 |
| 5. E. Franzio | 8:30AM | 3:00PM | $6 \frac{1}{2}$ | $6.80 | |
| 6. F. Galt | | 2:30PM | $7 \frac{1}{2}$ | $8.30 | $62.25 |
| 7. G. Hertz | 7:30AM | 3:30PM | 8 | | $54.00 |
| 8. H. Lee | 8:00AM | 6:00PM | | $4.25 | $48.50 |

*Using Information in a Table*

59

# Likely Letters

This is an activity for you and your family.

**WHAT LETTER OCCURS MOST OFTEN IN BOOKS?**

Write your guess here. _____

Now test your guess.
- Open any book.
- Pick out five sentences.
- Tally each letter below.

| Letter | Number of Times | Letter | Number of Times | Letter | Number of Times |
|---|---|---|---|---|---|
| A | | J | | S | |
| B | | K | | T | |
| C | | L | | U | |
| D | | M | | V | |
| E | | N | | W | |
| F | | O | | X | |
| G | | P | | Y | |
| H | | Q | | Z | |
| I | | R | | | |

1. Which letter occurred most often? _____

2. Which vowel occurred most often? _____

3. Which consonant occurred most often? _____

   Try again.
   - Use a different book.
   - Pick out five sentences.
   - Make another tally.

4. Did the same letter occur most often? _____

60     *Using Information in a Table*

NAME _____

# Tree Diagrams

**LESSON 30**

The Kendall Card Company makes cards in three shapes: circle, triangle, and rectangle.

The cards may be blue or yellow in color.

How many different cards can the Kendall Card Company make?

You can use a tree diagram to find out.

*For each shape there are 2 colors.*

```
     circle              triangle             rectangle
   /       \           /        \           /         \
 blue    yellow      blue     yellow      blue      yellow
```

The Bixby Block Company makes blocks in two shapes: sphere and cylinder.
The block may be red or brown in color.
The blocks may be large or small in size.

**1.** Complete the tree diagram to identify the different blocks that can be made.

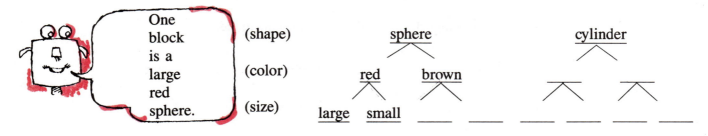

*One block is a large red sphere.*

(shape)

(color)

(size)

**2.** How many different blocks can the Bixby Block Company make? _____

**3.** How many of the blocks are red? _____

**4.** How many of the blocks are spheres? _____

**5.** How many of the blocks are large? _____

**6.** How many of the blocks are small and brown? _____

**7.** How many of the blocks are large cylinders? _____

**8.** How many of the blocks are red spheres? _____

*Using Tree Diagrams*

# Menu Matters

Plan some meals with your family. _____  _____  _____
Start with lunch.
   Identify three soups.
   Identify three sandwiches. _____  _____  _____

**1.** Use a tree diagram to find how
   many different lunches you can make.

(soup)

(sandwich) _____ _____ _____ _____ _____ _____ _____ _____ _____

**2.** How many different lunches can you make? _____

Now plan some dinners.

   Identify three main dishes. _____  _____  _____
   Identify two salads.
   Identify two desserts. _____  _____

**3.** Use a tree diagram to find how many different dinners you can make.

(main dish)

(salad)

(dessert) _____ _____ _____ _____ _____ _____ _____ _____ _____ _____ _____ _____

**4.** How many different dinners can you make? _____

*Using Tree Diagrams*

NAME _____

# Treasure Map

LESSON 31

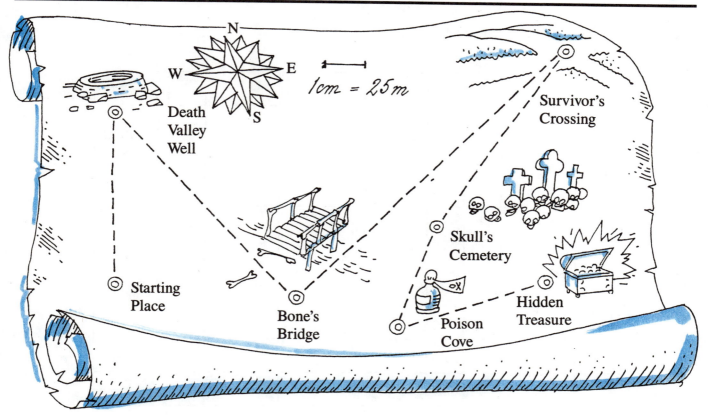

Use a centimeter ruler and the map to answer each question.
Stay on the roads.

**1.** What is the actual distance from Bone's Bridge to Survivor's Crossing? _____

**2.** What is the actual distance from Starting Place to Death Valley Well? _____

**3.** What is the actual distance from Skull's Cemetery to the Hidden Treasure? _____

**4.** Lonesome Lake is 275 m east of Starting Place. On the map, how many centimeters would Lonesome Lake be from Starting Place? _____

**5.** What is the actual distance from Bone's Bridge to Poison Cove? _____

**6.** What is the actual distance from the Starting Place to the Hidden Treasure? _____

*Using a Scale Drawing*

63

# Model Room

Have an adult help you with this project.
Pick a room in your house.
Make a scale drawing of the room on the grid paper below.
Mark the doorways.
Draw three pieces of furniture in the room.

Scale: ☐ stands for 1 square foot.

*Making a Scale Drawing*

# Enrichment MATH

## Grade 5
### Answer Key and Teaching Suggestions

AMERICAN EDUCATION PUBLISHING

# OVERVIEW

*ENRICHMENT MATH* was developed to provide children with additional opportunities to practice and review mathematical concepts and skills and to use these skills in the home. Children work individually on the first page of each lesson and then with family members on the second page. Every lesson presents high interest activities designed to heighten children's awareness of mathematical ideas and to enrich their understanding of those ideas.

*ENRICHMENT MATH* consists of 31 two page lessons at grade levels 1 through 6. At each grade level *ENRICHMENT MATH* covers all of the important topics of the traditional mathematics curriculum. Each lesson is filled with games, puzzles and other opportunities for exploring mathematical ideas.

# AUTHORS

**Peggy Kaye** is the author of *Games For Math* and *Games for Reading.* She spent ten years as a classroom teacher in New York City public and private schools, and is today a private tutor in math and reading.

**Carole Greenes** is Professor of Mathematics at Boston University. She has taught mathematics and mathematics education for more than 20 years and is a former elementary school teacher. Dr. Greenes is the author of a K-8 basal math series and has also written for programs such as *Reach Program, Trivia Math* and the *TOPS-Problem.*

**Linda Schulman** is Professor of Mathematics at Lesley College . For the past 12 years, she has taught courses in mathematics and mathematics education. Prior to her work at the college level, Dr. Schulman taught elementary school. She is the author of a basal mathematics textbook as well as of other curriculum programs including *TOPS-Problem Solving Program, The Mathworks* and *How to Solve Story Problems.*

# WHY ENRICHMENT MATH?

Enrichment and parental involvement are both crucial parts of children's education. More school systems are recognizing that this part of the educational process is crucial to school success. Enrichment activities give children the opportunity to practice basic skills and that encourages them to think mathematically. That's exactly the kind of opportunity children get when doing *ENRICHMENT MATH.*

One of the important goals of *ENRICHMENT MATH* is to increase children's involvement in mathematics and mathematical concepts. When children are involved in mathematics activities, they become more alert and receptive to learning. They understand more. They remember more. Games, puzzles, and "hands-on" activities that lead to mathematical discoveries are guaranteed to get children involved in mathematics. That's why such activities form the core of each *ENRICHMENT MATH* lesson.

Another important goal of *ENRICHMENT MATH* is to provide opportunities for parents to become involved in their children's education. Every *ENRICHMENT MATH* lesson has two parts. First, there is a lesson that the children do on their own. Second, there is a game or an activity that the child does with an adult. *ENRICHMENT MATH* doesn't ask parents to teach children. Instead the program asks parents to play math games and engage in interesting math activities with their children.

Published in 1995 by AMERICAN EDUCATION PUBLISHING
© 1991 SRA/McGraw-Hill

# HOW TO USE ENRICHMENT MATH

Each *ENRICHMENT MATH* book consists of 31 lessons on perforated sheets. On the front of each sheet, there is an activity that the child completes independently. On the back there is a follow-up activity for the child to complete with an adult. These group activities include games, projects, puzzles, surveys and trivia quizzes. The front and back pages of a lesson focus on the same mathematical skill.

Activities may be done at the time the skills are being taught to provide additional practice, or used at a later date to maintain skill levels.

Within each book, the lessons are organized into four or five sections. These sections correspond to the major mathematical topics emphasized at the particular grade level. This means you can quickly locate a lesson on whatever topic you want at whatever level is appropriate for your child. Let's say your first-grader is working on addition in school. You can feel confident that the first several lessons in the addition and subtraction section will have something suited to your needs.

---

## Also Available—ENRICHMENT READING

### Overview

*ENRICHMENT READING* is designed to provide children with practice in reading and to increase their reading abilities. The program consists of six books, one each for grade levels 1 through 6. The major areas of reading instruction—word skills, vocabulary, study skills, and literary forms—are covered as appropriate at each level.

*ENRICHMENT READING* provides a wide range of activities that target a variety of skills in each instructional area. The program is unique because it helps children expand their skills in playful ways with games, puzzles, riddles, contests, and stories. The high-interest activities are informative and fun to do.

Home and parental involvement is important to any child's success in school. *ENRICHMENT READING* is the ideal vehicle for fostering home involvement. Every lesson provides specific opportunities for children to work with a parent, a family member, an adult, or a friend.

LOOK FOR *ENRICHMENT READING* and *ENRICHMENT MATH* at stores that carry Master Skills.

## Also Available from American Education Publishing—

## BRIGHTER CHILD™ SOFTWARE

The Brighter Child™ Software series is a set of innovative programs designed to teach basic reading, phonics, and math skills in a fun and engaging way to children ages 3 - 9.

**Muppet™/Brighter Child™ Software available on CD-ROM**

| | |
|---|---|
| *Same & Different | Sorting & Ordering |
| *Letters: Capital & Small | Thinking Skills |
| *Beginning Sounds: Phonics | Sound Patterns: More Phonics |

*also available on diskette

**Brighter Child™ Software available on CD-ROM and diskette**

| | | |
|---|---|---|
| Math Grade 1 | Math Grade 2 | Math Grade 3 |
| Reading Grade 1 | Reading Grade 2 | Reading Grade 3 |

●**call (800) 542-7833 for more information**

**Brighter Child™ Software** Available at Stores Near You

# TEACHING SUGGESTIONS
## Grade 5
## Optional Activities

## A TIP FOR SUCCESS

Your student will find *ENRICHMENT MATH* Grade 5 assignments enjoyable and easy to understand. Although each lesson has simple and easy-to-read instructions, you may wish to spend a few minutes explaining some lessons before assigning the material. You might even do some of the activities prior to giving the assignments. Many of the activities can liven up an at-home math session and will prepare your child for even greater success.

### Part One: Place Value and Operations with Whole Numbers

Students are expected, by this grade level, to have mastered their basic addition, subtraction, multiplication, and division facts, although there are always a number who have not done so and a greater number who would benefit from additional practice. *ENRICHMENT MATH* Grade 5 devotes the first seven lessons to operations with whole numbers.

The activities in these lessons are designed to make practice with basic operations on whole numbers interesting if not fun. Some of the acitivities can be used not only at the beginning of the year but also throughout the year to practice and maintain skills. The activity *Palindromes*, for example, can be used throughout the year by simply writing a number and asking your child to use addition to find the palindrome. You might use this activity at the beginning of a math session or anytime there are a few extra minutes in the day. The game *The Big Difference* is another activity that can be pursued any time during the year by children who need additional practice with subtraction.

A lesson that provides practice in addition and division is the one entitled *Average Facts*. The lesson also helps children learn how to gather, organize, and report data. After this lesson has been utilized, you may wish to suggest that your child work on projects involving the same skills. For example, you can suggest that your child find the average length of a forearm (from the elbow to the tip of the fingers) in the family or find the average number of students in a classroom in their school.

Because place value is an important concept in all computational work with whole numbers, you may wish to develop variations of the game *Pick and Score*. For example, each player draws 4 of the 9 cards and then forms the greatest and least numbers possible. Practice with computation could be included if, in each case, they find the difference between the two numbers. The winner could be either the one with the greatest difference or the one with least difference.

### Part Two: Operations with Fractions and Probability

The first lesson in this section provides activities related to a subskill involved in addition and subtraction of fractions and mixed numbers: finding or identifying equivalent mixed numbers and improper fractions. Then the next two lessons address the addition and subtraction of fractions without common denominators. Before assigning the activity *Boxing Fractions* for independent work you may wish to discuss the lesson. Begin by writing the numbers 1, 1, 3, and 3 and ask your child to use the numbers as numerators and denominators to name two fractions whose sum is $\frac{2}{3}$. ($\frac{1}{3} + \frac{1}{3} = \frac{2}{3}$) Then write the numbers, 1, 1, 2, and 4 and ask your child to use these numbers to name fractions who sum is $\frac{3}{4}$. Help your child see that the notion of equivalent fractions is involved in the exercise because the answer is $\frac{1}{2} + \frac{1}{4}$ since $\frac{2}{4} + \frac{1}{4} = \frac{3}{4}$.

The game *Toss a Fraction* is an example of many activities and games in *ENRICHMENT MATH* Grade 5 that can be performed throughout the year whenever time permits or you judge your child's need for such practice and maintenance. Additional cards for this particular game can be created, if you wish, but note that they must be multiples of 2 x 3.

Before assigning the last lesson in this section for independent work, make sure your child understand how to find probability. First, count the number of possible events that can occur. Then, count the number of desired events that can occur. Finally, use a fraction to show the probability: The number of desired events is the numerator and the number of possible events is the denominator. For example, when drawing a card from a deck of regular playing cards, the number of possible events is 52. The number of aces if 4. Therefore, the probability of drawing an ace is 4 out of 52, or ⁴⁄₅₂.

## Part Three: Decimals

The six lessons in this section include finding equivalent decimals for fractions, examining place-value concepts with decimals, and then adding, subtracting, multiplying and dividing decimals.

The game *Close to the Target* is a good activity to help develop an understanding of place value in decimals. The game will help your child recognize that the place-value pattern in decimals is the same as it is in whole numbers, and that the decimal point is not a place but a device used to identify the ones place in the decimal. The game should be played before introducing operations with decimals and can be repeated throughout the year whenever you determine that your child will benefit from the activity.

You may want to introduce the lesson *Missing Points* by writing a few multiplication exercises on a separate piece of paper, such as 3.21 x 7.14. Then demonstrate how, by multiplying only the whole number parts, $3 \times 7 = 21$, a good estimate of the product can be found. Finally, ask your child to explain how the estimate can be used to correctly place the decimal point in the product if the digits of the product in correct order are 2 2 9 1 9 4.

## Part Four: Measurement and Geometry

The first two of the six lessons in this section deal with metric units and customary units of measure respectively. The activity on *Body Measures* can be used to discuss the difference between a unit (anybody's foot) and a standard unit (a foot that is exactly 12 inches long). You might also discuss that all of the units mentioned in this activity are names of standard units, although some of them are seldom if ever used anymore by the average person.

The lessons on *Picture Puzzle* and *Size It* involve finding both the perimeter and the area of geometric figures to help children recognize important differences in these two measurements.

## Part Five: Problem Solving

The last six lessons in *Enrichment Math* Grade 5 deal with problem solving and provide many opportunities for children to use a variety of problem-solving strategies. You might wish to help your child recognize that there often is more than one way to solve a problem by using the first problem in *Drawing Conclusions* to illustrate. For example, you can suggest the strategy of acting it out by having family members of three different heights play the parts of Nicole, Kimberly, and Barbara. Another strategy that can be used is draw a picture. Your child can draw vertical lines to represent the three people in the problem. Guess and check is a third possible strategy where your child might guess either Barbara or Kimberly as the taller and then check to see if this leads to any contradiction. Note that guess and check, because it is an important and useful strategy for solving many real-life problems, is given specific attention in the second lesson in this section.

The remaining lessons deal with problems where data is supplied in tables, graphs, and in maps or scale drawings. The lesson on *Tree Diagrams* helps children learn a procedure to use when the question involves a number of choices.

# Answer Key
## Grade 5–ENRICHMENT MATH

page 3:
1. 486+593=1079
2. 795+6201=6996
3. 9432+9=9441
4. 3268+78=3346
5. 826+7321=8147
6. 2047+5177=7224
7. 3428+6590=10,018
8. 37+68942=68,979
9. 84926+485=85,411
10. 3286+53216=56,502
11. 1047+39520=40,567
12. 26439+38643=65,082

page 4: answers will vary
answers will vary. Ex. pop, tot, mom, dad

page 5: 1. 170  2. 3,857  3. 12,496
4. 8,341  5. 21,598  6. 35,251
7. 45,027  8. 72,746

page 6: answers will vary

page 7: 1. A; 5408  2. A; 1036  3. A; 5400
4. A; 1626  5. B; 13,707
6. C; 28,905  7. B; 12,614
8. C; 27,435  9. D; 32,784
10. D; 31,056  11. A; 5932
12. B; 15,365

page 8: answers will vary

page 9:

| 1,1 | 2,2 | 3 | 3,7 | 5 | 0 | | |
|---|---|---|---|---|---|---|---|
| 1, | , | 0 | , | 1 | , | 4,4 | 8 |
| 5,2 | 0 | 9 | 1 | 6,6 | 6 | , | 8 |
| , | , | , | 7,7 | 8 | , | 8,8 | 9,9 |
| 10,2 | 0 | 6 | 7 | 0 | , | , | 4 |
| 11,6 | 0 | , | 12,4 | 0 | 7 | 5 | 2 |
| , | 7 | , | , | 0 | , | , | 8 |
| 13,2 | 4 | 3 | , | 14,7 | 8 | 4 | |

page 10: answers will vary

page 11: 1. 39; 92; 9  2. 140; 71; 1
3. 143; 216; 1  4. 105; 325; 5

page 12: answers will vary

page 13: 1. 3; T  2. 40; A  3. 13; I
4. 72; L  5. 31; B  6. 87; A
7. 22; C  8. 58; K

page 14: answers will vary

page 15:

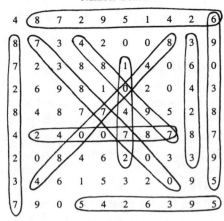

page 16: answers will vary

page 17: 1. $\frac{5}{3}$ New Delhi  2. $\frac{11}{5}$ Paris
3. $\frac{27}{8}$ Madrid  4. $\frac{11}{6}$ Oslo
5. $\frac{13}{7}$ Buenos Aires  6. $\frac{11}{4}$ Tokyo
7. $\frac{10}{3}$ Budapest  8. $\frac{25}{6}$ Athens
9. $\frac{9}{5}$ Rome  10. $\frac{15}{7}$ Canberra
11. $\frac{23}{8}$ Peking

page 18: answers will vary

page 19: 1. $\frac{1}{2}+\frac{1}{3}$  2. $\frac{1}{2}+\frac{3}{4}$  3. $\frac{1}{3}+\frac{1}{5}$  4. $\frac{3}{5}+\frac{1}{10}$
5. $\frac{2}{3}+\frac{3}{4}$  6. $\frac{1}{4}+\frac{9}{10}$  7. $\frac{1}{6}+\frac{7}{8}$  8. $\frac{5}{6}+\frac{2}{9}$

page 20: answers will vary

page 21:

1.

| $\frac{7}{8}$ | − | $\frac{3}{8}$ | = | $\frac{1}{2}$ |
|---|---|---|---|---|
| − | | − | | − |
| $\frac{1}{4}$ | − | $\frac{1}{8}$ | = | $\frac{1}{8}$ |
| = | | = | | = |
| $\frac{5}{8}$ | − | $\frac{1}{4}$ | = | $\frac{3}{8}$ |

2.

| $\frac{9}{10}$ | − | $\frac{2}{5}$ | = | $\frac{1}{2}$ |
|---|---|---|---|---|
| − | | − | | − |
| $\frac{3}{10}$ | − | $\frac{1}{5}$ | = | $\frac{1}{10}$ |
| = | | = | | = |
| $\frac{3}{5}$ | − | $\frac{1}{5}$ | = | $\frac{2}{5}$ |

3.

| $\frac{2}{3}$ | − | $\frac{1}{5}$ | = | $\frac{7}{15}$ |
|---|---|---|---|---|
| − | | − | | − |
| $\frac{2}{5}$ | − | $\frac{1}{15}$ | = | $\frac{1}{3}$ |
| = | | = | | = |
| $\frac{4}{15}$ | − | $\frac{2}{15}$ | = | $\frac{2}{15}$ |

4.

| $\frac{3}{4}$ | − | $\frac{1}{3}$ | = | $\frac{5}{12}$ |
|---|---|---|---|---|
| − | | − | | − |
| $\frac{1}{2}$ | − | $\frac{1}{6}$ | = | $\frac{1}{3}$ |
| = | | = | | = |
| $\frac{1}{4}$ | − | $\frac{1}{6}$ | = | $\frac{1}{12}$ |

page 22: answers will vary
page 23: 1. 13  2. 4  3. 15  4. 10  5. 100
6. 102  7. 52  8. 144  9. 755
10. 275
page 24: answers will vary
page 25:

1.
| $\frac{1}{64}$ | $\frac{1}{32}$ | $\frac{1}{16}$ | $\frac{1}{8}$ | $\frac{1}{4}$ |
|---|---|---|---|---|
| $\frac{1}{16}$ | $\frac{1}{8}$ | $\frac{1}{4}$ | $\frac{1}{2}$ | 1 |
| $\frac{1}{4}$ | $\frac{1}{2}$ | 1 | 2 | 4 |
| 1 | 2 | 4 | 8 | 16 |
| 4 | 8 | 16 | 32 | 64 |

Multiply by $\frac{1}{4}$ / Multiply by 2

2.
| 50,000 | 10,000 | 2000 | 400 | 80 |
|---|---|---|---|---|
| 5,000 | 1000 | 200 | 40 | 8 |
| 500 | 100 | 20 | 4 | $\frac{4}{5}$ |
| 50 | 10 | 2 | $\frac{2}{5}$ | $\frac{2}{25}$ |
| 5 | 1 | $\frac{1}{5}$ | $\frac{1}{25}$ | $\frac{1}{125}$ |

Multiply by 10 / Multiply by $\frac{1}{5}$

3.
| 128 | 16 | 2 | $\frac{1}{4}$ | $\frac{1}{32}$ |
|---|---|---|---|---|
| 64 | 8 | 1 | $\frac{1}{8}$ | $\frac{1}{64}$ |
| 32 | 4 | $\frac{1}{2}$ | $\frac{1}{16}$ | $\frac{1}{128}$ |
| 16 | 2 | $\frac{1}{4}$ | $\frac{1}{32}$ | $\frac{1}{256}$ |
| 8 | 1 | $\frac{1}{8}$ | $\frac{1}{64}$ | $\frac{1}{512}$ |

Multiply by 2 / Multiply by $\frac{1}{8}$

4.
| $\frac{20}{27}$ | $\frac{10}{27}$ | $\frac{5}{27}$ | $\frac{5}{54}$ | $\frac{5}{108}$ |
|---|---|---|---|---|
| $2\frac{2}{9}$ | $1\frac{1}{9}$ | $\frac{5}{9}$ | $\frac{5}{18}$ | $\frac{5}{36}$ |
| $6\frac{2}{3}$ | $3\frac{1}{3}$ | $1\frac{2}{3}$ | $\frac{5}{6}$ | $\frac{5}{12}$ |
| 20 | 10 | 5 | $2\frac{1}{2}$ | $1\frac{1}{4}$ |
| 60 | 30 | 15 | $7\frac{1}{2}$ | $3\frac{3}{4}$ |

Multiply by $\frac{1}{3}$ / Multiply by $\frac{1}{2}$

page 26: 1. $\frac{8}{15}$  2. $\frac{2}{5}$  3. $\frac{1}{4}$  4. $1\frac{5}{9}$  5. $4\frac{1}{4}$
page 27: 1. $\frac{1}{9}$  2. $\frac{5}{9}$  3. $\frac{3}{9}$ or $\frac{1}{3}$  4. $\frac{8}{9}$  5. $\frac{4}{9}$
6. A  7. B  8. C  9. C  10. B
11. C  12. B

page 28: answers will vary
page 29: Column 1: 0.5; 0.25; 0.3; 0.04; 0.4
Column 2: 0.6; 0.75; 0.8; 0.46; 0.9
Column 3: 0.85; 0.18; 0.7; 0.02; 0.24
Column 4: 0.2; 0.1; 0.16; 0.15;
BECAUSE IT WILL SQUEAL
page 30: answers will vary
page 31: 1. 5.73  2. 72.4  3. 24.37
4. 2.86  5. 4.824  6. 3.275
page 32: answers will vary
page 33: 1. $\frac{0.009}{T}, \frac{0.057}{A}, \frac{0.231}{X}, \frac{0.406}{I}$
2. $\frac{0.007}{T}, \frac{0.01}{R}, \frac{0.082}{A}, \frac{0.299}{I}, \frac{0.6}{N}$
3. $\frac{0.001}{A}, \frac{0.004}{I}, \frac{0.005}{R}, \frac{0.016}{P}, \frac{0.018}{L},$
$\frac{0.097}{A}, \frac{0.107}{N}, \frac{0.871}{E}$

page 34: 0.003 MATCH; 0.01 LAWN MOWER; 0.012 SAFETY PIN; 0.02 CARPET SWEEPER; 0.029 BALL POINT PEN; 0.209 ZIPPER; 0.294 AIR CONDITIONING; 0.412 AUTOMATIC TOASTER; 0.42 LONG PLAYING RECORD

page 35:

1.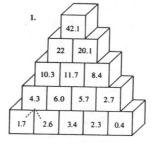

2.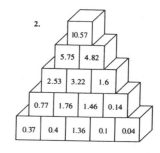

3.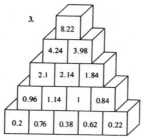

4.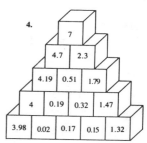

page 36: answers will vary
page 37: 1. 18.2  2. 10.3  3. 17.6
4. 377.25  5. 3.14  6. 167.2
7. 28.98  8. 142.1  9. 139.46
10. 1.17  11. 1.8  12. 1.74
13. 34.06  14. 25.6  15. 429.8
16. 302.6  17. 1867.32  18. 59.1
19. 4.488  20. 76.255
page 38: answers will vary
page 39: 1. 3; 1.2  2. 2; 1.2  3. 5; 1.2  4. 6; 1.2  5. 4; 1.2  6. 7; 1.2  7. 2; 2.41
8. 9; 2.41  9. 5; 2.41  10. 6; 2.41
11. 8; 2.41  12. 3; 2.41
page 40: 1. 203.1  2. 15.43  3. 122.1
4. 68.4  5. 9.69  6. 139.4
7. 7.08  8. 8.12  9. 11.17; 100.9
page 41: 1. 6; 3  2. 16; 8  3. 8; 4  4. 10; 5
5. 18; 9  6. 14; 7  7. 28; 14

71

page 42:

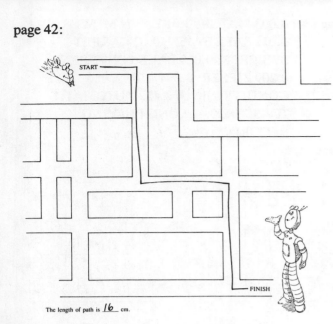

The length of path is 16 cm.

page 43: 1. =  2. >  3. >  4. <
5. =  6. <  7. =  8. >
9. >  10. <  11. <  12. =
13. >  14. >  15. =
16. >

page 44: answers will vary

page 45: 1. 2; 1  2. 1; 3  3. 4; 1  4. 3; 3
5. 6; 3  6. 8; 1

page 46: answers will vary. Possible answers given.

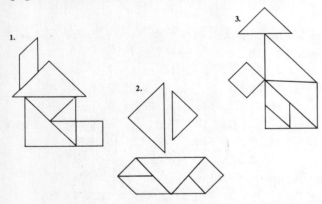

page 47: 1. Ben  2. Sara  3. Jack  4. Rosa
5. Mele  6. Elliot

page 48: answers will vary

page 49: 1. B;  2. D  3. A  4. C  5. E

page 50: answers will vary

page 51: 1. 6; 0; 0  2. 2; 4; 0  3. 0; 3; 2
4. 6; 4; 0  5. 3; 4; 2  6. 2; 5; 2

page 52: answers will vary

page 53: 1. Barbara  2. Saturday  3. Jon
4. 5 years old  5. $4.50  6. squash
7. 1:00pm  8. Tricia

page 54: answers will vary

page 55: 1. 14; 35  2. 28; 23  3. $\frac{14}{19}$; 23
4. 35; $\frac{28}{23}$  5. $\frac{14}{35}$; 19  6. $\frac{14}{19}$ ÷ 23; $\frac{28}{35}$

page 56:

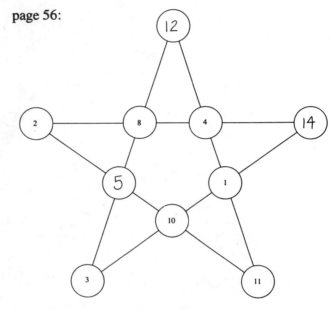

page 57: 1. Entertainment  2. Transportation
3. School Supplies, Transportation
4. Savings, Food, Entertainment
5. $6  6. $9  7. $10.50  8. $10.50
9. $162

page 58: answers will vary

page 59: 1. 3:00pm  2. $27.00  3. $6.40
4. 4  5. $44.20  6. 7:00am
7. $6.75  8. 10

page 60: answers will vary

page 61: 1.

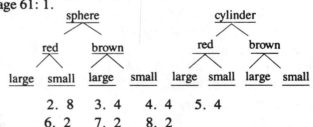

2. 8  3. 4  4. 4  5. 4
6. 2  7. 2  8. 2

page 62: 1. answers will vary.  2. 9
3. answers will vary  4. 12

page 63: 1. 250cm  2. 125m  3. 175m
4. 11cm  5. 475m  6. 875m

page 64: answers will vary